YPSILANTI DISTRICT LIB.

7101 9100 133 218 0

WITHDRAWN

D1301156

YPSILANTI DISTRICT LIBRARY

WITHDRAWN

John
CABOT

J
921
Cabot

FEB 1 7 2000

TELL ME ABOUT

John CABOT

by John Malam

Ypsilanti District Library
229 W. Michigan Ave.
Ypsilanti, MI 48197

Carolrhoda Books, Inc. / Minneapolis

This edition first published in the United States in 1999 by
Carolrhoda Books, Inc.

Copyright © 1997 by Evans Brothers Limited
First published in England in 1997 by Evans Brothers Limited, London

All U.S. rights reserved. No part of this book may be reproduced, stored in a
retrieval system, or transmitted in any form by an means, electronic,
mechanical, photocopying, recording, or otherwise, without the prior
written permission of Carolrhoda Books, Inc., except for the inclusion of
brief quotations in an acknowledged review.

Carolrhoda Books, Inc., c/o The Lerner Publishing Group
241 First Avenue North, Minneapolis, Minnesota 55401 U.S.A.

Website address: www.lernerbooks.com

Library of Congress Cataloging-in-Publication Data

Malam, John.
   John Cabot / John Malam.
      p. cm. — (Tell me about)
   Includes index.
   Summary: A biography of the Italian explorer who made several
voyages of discovery for England including the discovery of the
North American mainland in 1497.
   ISBN 1–57505–365–9 (alk. paper)
   1. Cabot, John, d. 1498 — Juvenile literature 2. Explorers—Italy—
Biography—Juvenile literature [1. Cabot, John, d. 1498. 2. Explorers.]
I. Title. II. Series: Tell me about (Minneapolis, Minn.)
   G370.C32M35 1999
   970.01′7′09—dc21
   [b]   98–8488

Printed by Graficas Reunidas SA, Spain
Bound in the United States of America
1 2 3 4 5 6 – OS – 04 03 02 01 00 99

John Cabot was an explorer. He lived such a long time ago that not much is known about him. No one even knows what he really looked like.

We do know that he was born in the 1450s, in a town in Italy. Some people think he came from a city called Genoa. Others say he was born near Naples. Both of these cities are near the sea.

This picture of John Cabot was painted around 1906. No one knows what he really looked like.

When John was born, his parents named him Giovanni Caboto. This was the name he was known by when he lived in Italy. Giovanni is the Italian name for John, and years later, when he lived in England, he changed his name to John Cabot.

This is a drawing of how Genoa looked in John's time.

John's last name may tell us something about his family. "Caboto" is related to Italian words meaning "near the coast." People were often named for the jobs they did, so John might have come from a family of sailors.

This is a photograph of modern Genoa. It is a busy port, just as it was in John's time.

When John was still a boy, he went to live in another part of Italy. He moved to the city of Venice. It was a busy port with many boats and ships coming and going all the time.

Venice must have looked strange to John. It seemed to float on the sea. Its buildings were built on tiny islands. The islands were surrounded by the sea. People traveled by boat on canals instead of by roads, and there were bridges everywhere.

A picture of Venice, painted when John lived there

Modern Venice, Italy. People use small boats to travel along the city's canals.

John's son, Sebastian, as an old man. He was an explorer and sometimes traveled with his father.

John lived in Venice for many years. He married a woman from Venice. Her name was Mattea. John and Mattea had three sons. They were named Lewis, Sebastian, and Sancio.

Alexandria, a trading city in North Africa

John worked as a merchant. He sailed across the Mediterranean Sea to buy and sell goods.

John sailed in a little ship that had a crew of just a few men. He sailed from Venice to a city in North Africa called Alexandria.

In Alexandria John bought spices such as pepper, nutmeg, and cloves; brightly colored silks and cloth; and medicines. He took them back to Italy and sold them.

The goods came from Asia, which was mostly unknown to Europeans. Camels carried the goods to Alexandria across mountains and deserts.

People in Europe used spices to make their food last longer.

Silks and spices were carried across deserts by camels.

Pilgrims in Mecca. John probably went to Mecca disguised as a pilgrim.

    Merchants in Alexandria told John about places they had seen on their travels.

    John wanted to see one of these exciting places for himself. He decided to go to Mecca, a Muslim

holy city. He went in disguise because he was not a Muslim himself.

John returned safely to Venice. He wanted to learn all he could about Asia, the mysterious land of silks and spices. He learned about the travels of a man named Marco Polo. Marco Polo was an Italian traveler who had visited Asia long before John's time. Marco Polo's book about his journey was like a travel guide.

Marco Polo, a traveler from Venice who visited Asia. John Cabot knew about Marco Polo's travels in Asia.

By about 1490, John and his family moved to Valencia, a city in Spain. John had found work there.

A sailor named Christopher Columbus came to Valencia. He said he had reached Asia by sailing westward around the world. This had never been done before, and John didn't believe it was possible. Columbus's descriptions didn't sound like the lands Marco Polo had seen, either.

John was right. He had not reached Asia.

The land that Columbus reached was really the West Indies.

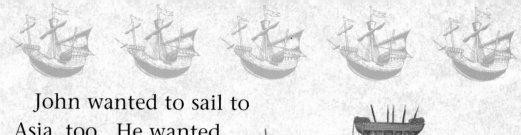

John wanted to sail to Asia, too. He wanted to bring back spices and silks. But a long voyage across the Atlantic Ocean would be expensive. He asked the kings of Spain and Portugal for money. Both kings refused to help him.

The first ships to cross the Atlantic Ocean were small. Sailors often had to sleep on the open deck.

John moved to England. He hoped someone there would pay for his voyage. The family settled in the city of Bristol. This was when John changed his name from Giovanni Caboto to John Cabot. It was easier for English people to say.

A coin from King Henry VII's time. King Henry gave John money for his voyage.

King Henry VII and the wealthy merchants of Bristol agreed to pay for John's voyage. They hoped he would bring valuable goods back from Asia that they could sell.

King Henry VII of England

On John's first voyage across the Atlantic Ocean, he ran out of food. He had to turn around and go back to England.

16

In May 1497, he tried the voyage again. With a crew of eighteen sailors, he sailed a small ship called the *Matthew*. After thirty-five days at sea, they reached land. John was sure this was Asia. He went ashore to explore. After one month sailing up and down the coast, John sailed back to Bristol with news of what he had seen.

A modern picture of the *Matthew,* the night before it left on its famous voyage

Newfoundland's main harbor

John became famous. He was called the "Grand Admiral." King Henry gave him a reward. People called John's land the "new-found land." They believed it was part of Asia.

But the land he had really found was North America. John Cabot was the first person from England to actually set foot on the mainland of North America. He may have landed on the large island of Newfoundland, which is part of Canada.

The next year, John set out again to the "new-found land," with a fleet of four or five ships. Only one ship came back. What happened to John Cabot and the other ships is a mystery. Nothing was ever heard of them again. Perhaps they sank in a storm. Perhaps they hit icebergs. Or perhaps they did reach land, but were unable to return. It was such a long time ago that no one will ever know what did happen.

A church window in Bristol, with pictures of John Cabot, his sons, and the *Matthew*

What happened to the *Matthew*? John's little ship did not go with him on his last voyage. Instead it became a transport ship, taking goods for many years to France and Ireland.

A modern copy of the *Matthew* was built to sail to North America in 1997, exactly 500 years after John Cabot did.

Important Dates

The letter *c* before a date means "about."

c.1450	Giovanni Caboto was born in Italy
c.1460	Went to live in Venice, Italy
c.1482–84	Married Mattea, a woman from Venice
1480s	Sons Lewis, Sebastian, and Sancio were born
1480s	Sailed ships in the Mediterranean Sea
1480s	Traveled to Mecca
c.1490	Went to live in Valencia, Spain
1492	Christopher Columbus sailed from Spain across the Atlantic Ocean. He landed in the West Indies, which he thought was in Asia
1493–95	Giovanni Caboto and his family moved to Bristol, England. He changed his name to John Cabot
1496	King Henry VII and the merchants of Bristol paid for him to go on a voyage in search of Asia
1496	First voyage ended in failure
1497	Reached North America in the *Matthew*
1498	Died while on his third voyage
1997	A modern copy of the *Matthew* was built to sail to Newfoundland, Canada

Key Words

Atlantic Ocean
the second largest ocean in the world

canal
a waterway used for transport

merchant
someone who buys and sells goods

port
a place that ships sail from

Index

Acknowledgments

The author and publisher gratefully acknowledge the following for permission to reproduce copyrighted material:

Cover Detail from *The Departure of John Cabot on his Voyage of 1497,* painted by Ernest Board in 1906. City of Bristol and Museum and Art Gallery/Bridgeman Art Library **Title page** John Cabot's ship the *Matthew,* painted by Bill Bishop, The Matthew Project **page 5** City of Bristol and Museum and Art Gallery/Bridgeman Art Library **page 6** AKG Photo **page 7** Guido Alberto Rossi/Image Bank **page 8** AKG/Erich Lessing **page 9** (top) Simon Harris/Robert Harding Picture Library (bottom) Peter Newark's Historical Pictures **page 10** (top left) Mary Evans Picture Library (bottom) Simon Westcott/Robert Harding Picture Library **page 11** Roger Stowell/Robert Harding Picture Library **page 12** Mohamed Amin/Robert Harding Picture Library **page 13** Biblioteca Nazionale, Turin/Bridgeman Art Library **page 14** (left) Gavin Hellier/Robert Harding Picture Library (right) AKG **page 15** Mary Evans Picture Library **page 16** (left) Christie's, London/Bridgeman Art Library (right) e.t. archive **page 17** The Matthew Project **page 18** David W. Hamilton/Image Bank **page 19** Mike Stannard/St Mary Redcliffe Church, Bristol **page 20** (main photo) Colin Sanger (inset) Max Mudie/The Matthew Project

About the Author

John Malam has a degree in ancient history and archeology from the University of Birmingham in England. He is the author of many children's books on topics that include history, natural history, natural science, and biography. Before becoming a writer and editor, he directed archeological excavations. Malam lives in Manchester, England, with his wife, Hilary, and their children, Joseph and Eve.